Special Pants

Childish Poems for Adults

Richard Coletta

Publishing Partners
Port Townsend, WA 98368
www.marciabreece.com

Printed in the United States of America

Cover art by Virginia Ashby

ISBN 978-1-944887-47-6
eISBN: 978-1-944887-49-0

Contents

Bzzzzzz

Today I went to mow the lawn and realized I was not
    alone.
Amid the dandelions and grass, every time I made a
    pass
trying to de-weed my yard, I realized I had to guard
    against my mower
running over something hiding in the clover . . .
    something I could barely see,
no bigger than a goober pea—a tiny little bumble bee.
He just kept looking up at me—following me all
    around, wandering up and down there
close to the ground, making that sound.
His buzzing had a certain tone—"Leave my dandelions
    alone" he seemed to shout,
as close as I could figure out.

It seems these last ten years or so, for reasons I don't
    really know,
I've stopped just swatting bees (and spiders).
I must admit that I've provided spider rides—that's
    how I guided them outside,
in little jars to my back yard to set them free. It just
    makes perfect sense to me.

Perhaps it is a little Zen of me, to be considerate of a
    bee, but not to be seems just so wrong.
It never really takes that long to help them in their
    small requests.
How're you supposed to treat your guests?

Well, to get back to my new mown lawn . . . I have to
    say, it does look wrong.
In trying to appease the bees, I may have taken
    liberties.
My lawn may look like a jigsaw puzzle . . .
but I'm glad it's filled with bumble bee buzzle.

8/26/12

Special Pants

It's under where? It's under there . . .
Beneath your gown or somewhere down
Below your suit or pair of pants
(The ones in which you might have ants)

Of course I mean the place you sit
The only place that they could fit . . .
The place that's already been chosen
If you don't want your assets frozen

Heaven knows that some have tried
To wear their special clothes—outside
Which doesn't really fit the norm . . .
Unless you have a "special" form

They have to be put on just right
Not too baggy, not too tight
So you don't have to use your hands
They're made with special rubber bands
To guarantee that you don't lose
Your special pants down by your shoes

Of course you may have just forgot
To put them on, but that would not
Make any explanation easy . . .
Some might even call you sleazy

If they should get stuck in the middle
Any little kid'll fiddle
Trying to attain relief . . .
I know, you're saying, let's be brief

Alright, I say this all in jest
But don't forget to wear your best
Remember what your mother meant . . .
In case you're in an accident

5/16/02

Roughage

Sometimes I eat my veggies in my underwear
I don't care what people say when they point and stare
I think it's very apropos that you should get your
    roughage
By being very natural and showing off your buffage

6/1/12

It's Not

Oh, it looked like a booger but it wasn't
Just sitting on the shoulder of my cousin
I was sure he just forgot to wipe the tiny little dot away
That I thought was a booger, but it's not

4/8/09

Hamsters

Hamsters come and hamsters go
They run and they run and they don't even know
That their home is a cage and their life isn't real
They're just running in place inside a toy wheel

Someone should tell them, go to the trouble
To warn them that their Paradise is just a big bubble
It certainly seems like the right thing to do
Though they do seem so happy . . . I'll leave it up to you

4/22/16

Dad

My father was an idiot, but then, whose father isn't?
I told him I knew EVERYTHING . . . he said, he knew
    I didn't
All he ever said to me was, "Go clean up your messes"
He also said, "I'm glad you didn't end up wearing
    dresses"
True story

1/6/17

BOYS

Boys are pigs, every girl knows.
They push and grab and blow their noses at the table.
They jab and pick and poke with a stick, and won't
    ever give you an ice cream lick.
They're rude and crude and sometimes lewd . . . they
    always like to use the word "nude".
They never ever chew their food.
They pop your bubble gum bubble and always seem to
    be in trouble.
They fight and yell and scream and curse and I can't
    think of anything worse . . .

Except when they ask you to the dance, and then they
    wear their shabby pants,
and hang around with all the guys . . . and stand
    around and tell their lies,
and make believe that you're not there, or stand with
    their mouths' open and stare
at other girls they might have missed . . . .

I wonder if I'll ever get kissed?

8/27/12

Naked

Naked is wonderful, naked is fine
You can't take it away from me, naked is mine
Naked is perfect, naked is true
Naked is the real honest to goodness you
Naked is skinny, naked is fat
Naked is any variation between this and that
Naked is natural, naked is simple
No one really cares if you have a pimple
Naked is real and can be terribly fun
If you just remember not to leave your stuff in the sun
Naked is easy and naked is quick
Especially if you're interested in seeing someone else's
Grooming standards in their nether regions

3/3/17

Boing!

There's a spider in my bathroom, crawling up the wall
I've always wondered how they do that—they hardly
        ever fall
Reserved yet industrious, with hands and legs to spare
I'm sure they could juggle twenty little balls in the
        air—without a care!
Upside down sideways, swinging or swaying
They always make it look like they're just playing
I know from my science class they mostly look for
        food
But so often they just hang there with that look of
        "Hey Dude!"
They're never in a hurry to get where they're going
Except maybe when a tasty fly makes their web go
        "BOING!"

12/12/14

Silly Fun

Silly and Fun are never the ones to turn a smile into a
    frown
But they're the first ones to giggle, as they waggle and
    wiggle
Towards the bottom of the hill they both roll down

2/12/16

Cacophony

Cacophony sounds like a very LOUD word
But one I'm not sure that everyone has heard
If used in a sentence though, I'm sure you would find
That it conjures up just what you hear in your mind

4/6/15

Ode To A Hog

Harley a Davidson goes by that I don't think about my
    motorcycle.

10/5/05

Mining

Everything I write is not a gem of polished gold
My work is simply making something new of
    something old

5/28/16

Dog Lover's Lament

Oh, how I hate you, you pile of poo
I collect you and bag you—what else can I do?
If left where you lie, no one can deny
You'd collect every fly in the sky—ew!

Now if I don't address you, we all know the mess
You will make at some later date
With your uncanny adherences, your second
      appearances
It's no wonder so many think—it's just fate

You know I'm not playing here
You know what I'm saying here
But I can whisper—I don't have to shout
Shhh—it happens to the best of us
And even the rest of us
We all inevitably scream your name . . . .
Cause there's never anyone else around to blame

5/15/16

Grooming

Some hair is barely there
Some hair is everywhere
But if you find that you don't mind
Then you don't need hair care

4/10/16

Bad Dreams

Poisonous snakes hide in my dreams
I really believe they like hearing my screams
But it seems so absurd 'cause the snakes aren't real
And why would they even care how I feel?

12/31/16

Sitting

I believe my lawn really likes to be mowed
And that little boats sitting would rather be rowed
And what respectable garden doesn't want to be hoed?
Do they just speak to me or is it some secret code?

So I trim and I paddle, I garden and I hear
These voices keep calling-their message seems clear
"Don't give up on us now, we're not ready to quit
We're just tired of sitting here . . . watching you sit"

6/25/17

Manners

I rarely make my bed up, but mostly wipe my feet
I almost always clean my plate every time I eat
I usually smile and tip my hat, try to watch my
    P's and Q's
And even though I was born in New Jersey, I try not to
    say "Youse"

I try not to worry or be in a hurry and I'll probably pet
    your pet, before we've even met
I hold doors open for almost everyone, but sometimes
    I forget
Nobody's perfect, but we can all try to do the best
    we can
By behaving better than some people in the news-
    whether a woman or a man

8/12/17

The Fast Lane

You won't get a ticket from the Word Constabulary
Because you're speeding to improve your vocabulary
They might give you an escort, or a 21-gun salute
Perhaps even an extension on your poetic license
    to boot
Your fondness for words, now turned to infatuation
 Might just be a clear cut case of alliteration

7/1/16

A Reflection

The heart of a poet
The eyes of a child
The hands of a tinker
A mind that runs wild

A look in the mirror
To find out what's true
Is it an illusion
Or is that really you?

We see what we want to
It might not be real
Sometimes it just
Depends how we feel

Familiar is cozy, adventure is fun
These days you wonder, which way will you run
Keep asking the questions, keep trying to find
The ultimate answer to, "What's on your mind?"

1/8/16

The Ride

I'm not ready for the junk heap
I'm not ready to lay down
I'm not ready to unwind and relax
Change from a verb—into a noun

I've still got some ideas cooking
I've still got some recipes
Don't suggest I acquiesce
Don't look for me on my knees

You'll find me in the thick of it
Wielding my sword as if it was new
Reaching up inside my sleeve
To show you, I still have a trick of two

I don't have to be in the spotlight now
I'm comfortable off to one side
To catch the brass ring is a very good thing
But I'm still enjoying the ride

7/26/16

TIPS

When I go in a restaurant, a diner, or cafe,
I want to get some value for the money I will pay
Pretty decorations on the walls, or on my plate
Give no clear indication to the hunger I must sate

I work hard for my money, and if I'm to pay a fee
I do not wish to bandy words with Mr. Maitre'd
I tell them when I first come in, I don't care who
    their boss is
It isn't for their menu, chef, or any fancy sauces

I have a gauge as old as time, that tells me where to sit
But every server serving food is not a perfect fit
It isn't for the pretty face, the curves or pouty lips
I always say I want the waitress with the biggest tips

6/28/12

Elephants

When I look through my binoculars, what do you
    think I see?
The great and mighty elephant, no bigger that a flea
I pick him up with tweezers small and place him in
    my bottle
I can't be sure how many will fit, but me, I think a lot'll

8/28/15 with nods to Richard Armour

Pigeons

Pigeons always dip and peck
They do that funny thing with their neck
Everybody knows they get no respect
But what if they dressed like penguins?

11/12/15

Driving

Did you forget how to drive? Did you ever really know?
I can't always control my involuntary horn blow
I do it for safety, and it's often automatic
It happens when my car nears an accident fanatic
Your reactions are awful, your decisions are worse
You're a bane to existence, you're just a speeding hearse!

7/1/16

Dreams

Are you dragging your ass from one day to the next?
Are you hoping that some donkey will send you a text
That'll blast into viral space and make you a star?
How's that gonna happen if you keep your dreams
        in a jar?

4/4/16

Baseball

I wish I had every baseball bat
I'd use my sander to make them all flat
I'd turn them all into the perfect bed slat
Then I'd sleep so much better . . . and that would be that

10/11/16

Words (My Mother Said to Me)

Don't touch pooh that doesn't belong to you!
Get your feet up off that couch, it isn't yours!
Never run with scissors! If you keep that up you'll get
    blisters!
And just remember—when it rains, it pours!

Go comb your hair! And sit up in that chair!
I've told you money doesn't grow on trees!
Don't yell down the street—and wipe your muddy feet!
And whatever happened to Thank You and Please?

There is no Santa Claus and I'm very sure because
I never got those things my letters asked for.
Just keep your eyes crossed like that, you'll go blind as
    a bat!
And your sweaty socks are leaving footprints on my
    clean floor!

Do what I say, not what I do! Turn the lights off when
    you're thru!
Because I said so! And at my door you take off those
    filthy shoes!
Don't make me come back there! Whoever said life
    was fair?
You just better learn to mind your P's and Q's!

Don't read in the dark! Don't make the dog bark!
And don't talk while I'm talking on the phone!
Is there something wrong with you? Were you raised
    in a zoo?
Just wait till your father gets home!

10/4/14

I Wonder

I wonder how I got here
I wonder who I am
Is this the way I'm supposed to be?
Should I be eating ham?

I wonder why the sky is blue
And what is right . . . or wrong
I wonder why I start to cry
When I hear a certain song

Should I be thinking things like this?
Should I go out and play?
Should I be listening to-or questioning
Everything you say?

I've heard it said, "You're better off dead"
And "Ignorance is bliss"
I'm going to have to figure this out for myself
I'm going to have to think about all this

I wonder all the things you do
Because you are just like me
I've just been told, you're 8 years old
They say I'm 63

5/15/16

Growing Up

First you knew a little
Then you knew a lot
Then you knew you didn't know much
Then you just forgot

8/15/16

Underwear

There was a pair of underwear just sitting on my bed
But when I turned around I found it on my puppy's
    head
I lose a lot of stuff like that, almost everything I own
Maybe my next pair of underwear, should be in the
    shape of a bone

4/4/16

Bears

The life of a bear in the woods can't be beat
Nothing too salty, nothing too sweet
But bring one home and prepare for the riot
You just might be an integral part of his diet

10/12/16

The Fly

The housefly is common and gets a bad rap
For it's everyday propensity to hang around crap
If I was a fly, I'd say, "Call me Dragon!"
Because, as they say, if it's true, it ain't braggin

4/10/16

I'm Just A Meat And Potatoes Guy

I'm not afraid to say that eating my cereal
With milk and fruit sometimes makes me delireal
Yes I love my veggies like I love my mom
But I've gotta say, meat and potatoes are just the bomb

You probably won't find me dancing all night
Shaking my booty till the dawn's early light
But if the meat and potatoes are smothered in gravy
You can bet your bottom dollar, my review will be ravy

6/6/16

Say That Again?

Put it in the hopper, drop it in the bin
Make sure you beat 'em, every time you win
Set it on the mantel, place it on the shelf
Talk about your growing ego, brag about yourself

Give 'em all the dickens, let 'em go to hell
This is how you sound the alarm when you ring
    the bell
Flip a Uey, turn around 180 degrees
Put this thing on ice for me, give it the deep freeze

Tell me how you got this far, gimme' the lowdown
Then you better hit the bricks, beat it outta' town
Lots of ways to say it, of course they're not all the same
Some might say synonymy . . . a rose by any other name

12/12/14

Sex

Every time I have a good idea, I want to go have sex . . .
Isn't that a good idea?

9/30/16

More Sex

Every time I think about sex
I remember that it's just something I did with my ex
I'm not in a position now where I can enjoy it
But you know what they say
You'll lose it if you don't employ it

5/18/02

Cab Driver's Motto

If everything's going your way, you just might be in
the wrong lane

6/94

Train of Thought

Just because you can see the light at the end of the tunnel
doesn't mean you're on the right track.

12/4/15

Bedtime

First I place my head between a pillow and the bed
Then another pillow stuck between my knees
Another pillow at my back to take up any blanket slack
Then a pillow on my body if you please

This might seem to be enough, but I would gladly
Take another puffy pillow and just hug it like a bear
They say there's always room for Jello, and I'm a very
    clever fellow
But as for pillows, I truly swear, I don't know where

6/6/16

Decorum

Squished boobs in a shirt, used strictly to flirt
Are an obvious offense to my eye
But what really makes me curse
And makes it much, much worse, is when I look up
And notice . . . it's a guy
It's confusing to us, we don't want to make a fuss
It's not just a matter of gender
I'm sure I'm not the first one, who, in liking a person
Just wanted to know . . . are you a receiver or a sender?

7/1/16

Spiders

I found a spider swimming pool
All lit up sparkly like a wedding jewel
The mirrored surface reflected the sun
While the clouds protected their splashing fun

A philodendron leaf provided a slithery ride
Down twisty tiers of slip and slide
I watched as they frolicked, playing their spidery games
Wondering if they all knew each other's names

Then the strangest thing happened when they noticed
    my gaze
They all lost their interest and resumed their old ways
It was frightening to witness the change that occurred
As if I was some dangerous spider eating bird

I hate that spiders have such rotten reputations
My guess is, it's just bad movie roles, and overactive
    imaginations

9/2/16

School

If you want to take your idea to fruition
You have to be willing to pay the tuition
If school isn't for you, well, don't let that block it
There are still other doors, but you'll have to hard
      knock it

7/2/16

Tools

When you are at work, don't act like a jerk
Just smile and say, "Have a nice day!"
But you have to mean what you say to me
I won't believe you if you're just buzzin' like a bee

Take a moment to enjoy who you are
You don't need to have a fancy souped-up car
It's fairly easy, just follow this rule
Be as nice as you can and don't act like a tool

7/21/16

The Humor of Logic

Two wrongs don't make a right . . . but three lefts do!

Notions

I'm not really sure if it's this way or that
It could have been a dog-or maybe even a cat
I can't really say if it was tall or short
Keep in mind, I'm not a professional, I just do this for
      sport

I could draw you a picture, if I just had my pen
If you'd seen it you'd understand perfectly then
But it happened so fast, in the blink of an eye
It was here, and then gone-I have no idea why

You might say they're ephemeral, if you know
      what I mean
Yes, it's another way of saying things aren't always
      what they seem
You believe that you're someplace, specific and clear
Then you squint your eyes for just a moment, and
      slowly "there" becomes "here"

I tell you I'm not schizophrenic or mentally unstable
But sometimes I want to crawl right under the table
Of course "under the table" could mean beneath the
      roots of a great oak tree
With a warren of scared rabbits desperately seeking a
      place to be free

Yes, there is a freedom in jumping from one place
      to the next
With a speed and agility you don't really possess
But it sometimes is frightening, and don't be misled
Because sometimes all this happens-while you're still
      in your bed

12/8/17

Little Pieces

Love

Love is the glue that binds the Universe . . .
but you still need a good Russian dressing to hold a
    Reuben together

Naturally

If you feel joy from being silly, even if you just do it
    willy nilly
If every William you call Billy, isn't that better than
    taking a pilly?

Silly Is

Silly is as silly does
If you have been, then you was
As birds will fly and bees will buzz
You sometimes have to, just because

Sometimes

Sometimes I forget to remember
Sometimes I think it's March in November
Sometimes I forget what I said
But somehow, I always remember when it's time
    for bed

Think

If you feel the itch, you scratch
In the dark, you light a match
When you're puzzled, here's the catch
Every idea needs to hatch

Fame

If you live in a cottage made of cheese
Writing silly poems that nobody reads
You have to be willing to take the blame
For the fact that nobody knows your name

The Diaper

I believe the word diaper is one of those words
That most would be willing to give to the birds

The most exercise I get is jogging my memory . . .

If You Can't Be Funny, Be Fun in D

If you can't be funny, be fun
Put a hamburger patty on a hot dog bun
Make a puppet with your socks, or a joke with
two knocks, If you can't be funny, be fun

There's a time for serious, a time for insane
But they're mostly, really, just about the same
Paint your face like a clock, have a Hickory
Daquiri Doc, If you can't be funny, be fun

Don't strain too hard, you'll have a heart attack
You can be the good guy and still be wearing black
If I sit on your lap, will you let me take a nap? If you
can't be funny, be fun

If you think it's two, but it's really only one
If it looks like a penguin, but it's just a nun
Don't be alarmed, I grew up on a farm, If you
can't be funny, be fun

I'll try to make this short and sweet
Make believe we just met on the street
I tip my hat to most everyone I meet, If you can't
be funny, be fun

I was walking down the street, just the other day
When the wind blew me over, chased my blues away
I was a basket case, but I found a parking space, If
you can't be funny, be fun

You can laugh like Seth Rogen, anytime you want
(heh heh heh)
You can say that you can't or you can say that
you can't
Just don't get caught with your panties in a knot,
If you can't be funny, be fun

Wear a big red nose or a fake mustache
You can quote Bill Shakespeare or Ogden Nash
Just spread a little cheer from ear to ear, If you
can't be funny, be fun

10/13/18

The Forest for The Trees in D

Everybody wants to be different, nobody wants to be
    the same
I just can't figure out the reason, a rose by any other
    name
Set your sights upon the horizon, unfurl your flags in
    the breeze
While you're tryin' to find what's on your mind, you
    can't see the forest for the trees

An original's better than a copy, though it's hard to
    find a perfect fit
A chair as solid as the Rock of Gibraltar, is bound to
    last a little bit
When you get up and look in the mirror, take a gander
    at what you see
You don't have to join an arm of the military, to be all
    that you can be

Don't take a nap on a railroad track, don't go wadin' in
    the sea
It's a bad decision to get a circumcision if you're
    trying' to find ecstasy
How many holes in a doughnut my friend? One'll just
    suit me fine
If you'd rather have a laugh than to take a bath, well
    ain't that a hell of a rhyme?

Always try to set a good example, don't let others bring
    you down
Don't get caught just sittin' on the sidelines, when you
    know you should be going to town
Don't just listen to the rhythm, try and figure out the
    meaning of the words
Ya' gotta be loyal to your own true self, otherwise it's
    just all for the birds

Everybody wants to be different, nobody wants to be
    the same
I just can't figure out the reason, a rose by any other
    name
Set your sights upon the horizon, unfurl your flags in
    the breeze
While you're tryin' to find what's on your mind, you
    can't see the forest for the trees

9/26/16

The Thrift Store Blues in C

I'm lookin' in the bottom of a cardboard box
Tryin' to find the keys for a bunch of old locks,
        I've been
Standin' here for hours but I figure, I just can't lose
'Cause when I find a bargain, I know I've got the
        Thrift Store Blues

Every Tuesday is Senior's Day
But if you're not old enough you have to pay
Much higher prices for these items that have been used
So you know where to find me, I'm learnin' 'bout the
        Thrift Store Blues

Oh don't try to tell me that's 100 years old
It's been here for three weeks 'cause it never sold as a
Junky old, lidded wooden box full of socks and
        old shoes
Now it's Shabby Chic at my house, that's the Thrift
        Store Blues

My sweetheart is searchin' through racks of women's
        clothes
For nice clean name brands and God only knows if
        that
Jacket doesn't fit her, then some Ebay bidder just
        won't refuse
'Cause she's figured out, how to use, the Thrift Store
        Blues
I'm standin' at the bargain bin sortin' through stuff
We've been here for hours I just can't get enough
        of this
Second hand, hand-me-down, downsizin' . . . ." Uh,
        what size are those shoes?"
Yes, I'm neck deep in refuse, singing' the Thrift
        Store Blues

The Poo Song (Ukelele in D)

You . . . never go poo . . . when I'm with you
You . . . don't want me . . . anywhere near you
There's . . . no need . . . for you to get upset
I . . . would never compromise . . . your toilette
I . . . really don't care . . . about your scent
I . . . like you better here . . . than if you went . . . away

It wouldn't put me in a coma
If I caught your aroma
So darling . . . you can poo . . . when I'm with you

I . . . don't know why . . . you are so shy
It's . . . not like I sniff . . . just to get high
I . . . always brag . . . about your beauty
But I . . . never say a word . . . about your duty
You . . . should always know . . . that I'm your friend
I . . . don't care about what happens in the end

It wouldn't put me in a coma
If I caught your aroma
So darling . . . you can poo . . . when I'm with you
It's ok to use the loo . . . when I'm with you

5/13/13

Don't Tell Me What To Do
(DTMWTD) in C

You like me and I like you, DTMWTD
I like me and you like you, DTMWTD
Take the floor out when you walk the dog
Saw like a baby when yer sleepin' like a log
Go get Pete he's a sinking' in the bog, but DTMWTD

I put some milk in yer coffee mug, DTMWTD
An eel just married a lightnin' bug, DTMWTD
If yer dull ya can't make a point
I don't wanna be the only singer in the joint
I hope yer not waitin' for a priest to anoint you, DTMWTD

There's too many Ollies and not enough Stans, DTMWTD
Life's what happens when yer makin' other plans, DTMWTD
Ya don't have to be so self-controlled
It doesn't always have to be Rock-n-Roll
The game's still fun even when ya miss a goal, DTMWTD

Don't hitch yer wagon to a falling star, and DTMWTD
If yer drivin' in the water then ya went too far, DTMWTD
Everybody's happy 'cause the gang's all here
Don't be cryin' over tears in your beer
Too many cooks in the kitchen make it clear, DTMWTD
Dilly dally ding dang doo

9/13/16

I Can't Stop My Leg

I stand on the same old corner every single day
Watchin' everybody walkin' their own separate way
They all think I'm crazy, been dropped on my head
I tell them the same old story, I can't stop my leg

I can't stop my leg (no, no)
I can't stop my leg (can't you see)
You can stop the music in me
But I can't stop my leg

You can push your pencils, or sell your Daily News
You can bite the hand that feeds or just express your views
You can call the president, a lyin' in your bed
But you can't stop the music in me, 'cause I can't stop my leg

I can't stop my leg (no, no)
I can't stop my leg (can't you see)
You can stop the music in me
But I can't stop my leg

12/12/85

Come Out and Play in C

My girl says she loves me, but tells me to stay away
She's got a lot of work to do, I'll just get in the way,
    she says
She knows that I'll distract her, from accomplishing
    her goals
But I can't help the way I feel about her, we're two
    kindred souls
I know I've heard this all before, I don't care what
    people say

Come out and play, come out and play, hey
I don't mean tomorrow, I'm talkin' 'bout today
Come out and play

They say that time is money, the early bird he gets
    the worm
In 50 years you'd think that was a lesson I could
    learn, I know
I try to be responsible and do just what I'm told,
    but then
That little voice inside me screams out, "Just go for
    the gold!"
Well, after all is said and done, there just may be
    hell to pay

Come out and play, come out and play, hey
I don't mean tomorrow, I'm talkin' 'bout today
Come out and play
Hip hip hooray, come out and play
Beg, steal or borrow what you need, but for today
Come out and play

11/15/12

It's Just Congeniality

I've fountains of frivolity
And mountains of "Oh golly gee!"
I am the best that I can be
And wear my heart right on my sleeve

It shouldn't be that hard for you
Just spreading cheer amongst the few
It seems the best that you can do
If I can do it, you can to

So grab a smile and join the fun
You shouldn't be the only one
Just start off slow and then you run
You'll get the feel before you're done

So follow me to left or right
Don't let me get out of your sight
In shadow or in broad daylight
It's easy to do this all night

I'm running out of pressure now
But you can see exactly how
This isn't just a sacred cow
And when you're done you just say "Wow!"

3/19/18

Wiggle Waggle

You can close your eyes . . . when you Wiggle Waggle
Look up to the skies . . . when you Wiggle Waggle
Wriggle like a fish . . . when you Wiggle Waggle
Make a secret wish . . . when you WiggleWaggle

If you live on a farm . . . you can Wiggle Waggle
You should do no harm . . . when you Wiggle Waggle
Sit and count your toes . . . when you Wiggle Waggle
Everybody knows . . . how to Wiggle Waggle

Life is not so bad . . . when you Wiggle Waggle
You don't have to be sad . . . when you Wiggle Waggle
Let's get some ice cream . . . then we'll Wiggle Waggle
It feels just like a dream . . . when you Wiggle Waggle

Babies always coo . . . when you Wiggle Waggle
You were born to do . . . the Wiggle Waggle
Don't forget to smile . . . when you Wiggle Waggle
Try it for a while . . . it's just a Wiggle Waggle

This is simply called . . . the Wiggle Waggle
Don't be afraid to fall . . . as you Wiggle Waggle
Bunnies when they hop . . . do the Wiggle Waggle
Every Mom and Pop . . . needs to Wiggle Waggle

Even when you walk . . . you can Wiggle Waggle
You don't have to talk . . . when you Wiggle Waggle
Roll right down a hill . . . as you Wiggle Waggle
Its better than a pill . . . if you Wiggle Waggle

Angels always fly . . . when they Wiggle Waggle
Wave as you go by . . . when you Wiggle Waggle
Such a simple thing . . . this little Wiggle Waggle
You're allowed to sing . . . when you Wiggle Waggle

You can use your hands . . . when you Wiggle Waggle
You can sit or stand . . . when you Wiggle Waggle
You can even jiggle . . . when you Wiggle Waggle
Hope it doesn't tickle . . . when you Wiggle Waggle

It's an easy pace . . . when you Wiggle Waggle
Make a funny face . . . when you Wiggle Waggle
Isn't it just fine . . . when you Wiggle Waggle
I do it all the time . . . I just Wiggle Waggle

It always feels so good . . . when you Wiggle Waggle
And you knew it would . . . when you Wiggle Waggle
Just take off your shoes . . . when you Wiggle Waggle
Chase away your blues . . . when you Wiggle Waggle

I can't seem to stop . . . going Wiggle Waggle
I just saw a cop . . . do the Wiggle Waggle
Monkeys in the trees . . . like to Wiggle Waggle
Just do as you please . . . as you Wiggle Waggle

10/12/13

Old White Guys in Ties

They say they're gonna fix everything up, "make
    America great again"
Build a wall to protect us all, they say they've got a
    brand new plan
But I feel like I've heard these words before, just stated
    in a different way
So I took a little look in my History book, and here's
    what it had to say

Don't believe everything you hear my friend, There's a
    sucker born every single minute
There's nothing up my sleeve, Ya just gotta believe—
    This isn't gonna hurt a bit
You can have your cake and eat it too, It's better if it's
    super-sized
Old white guys in ties keep telling me lies, why am
    I so surprised

If you say little is huge, well, that's subterfuge, it just
    doesn't make a lot of sense
If big is small we should all be appalled by your lack
    of intelligence
When a thief in the night becomes a thief in the light,
    that's drawing a line in the sand
If you use your best words and it still smells like a
    turd, that's the time we need to make a stand

Don't believe everything you hear my friend, There's a
    sucker born every single minute
There's nothing up my sleeve, Ya just gotta believe,
    This isn't gonna hurt a bit
You can have your cake and eat it too, It's better if it's
    super-sized
Old white guys in ties keep telling those lies, why am
    I so surprised

1/27/17

Evil Smells

There seems to be no reason, and certainly no rhyme
To the line of bull that's spewing out of D.C. all the time
It used to be occasional, some bad news here and there
It's just a giant pile now, and the smell is everywhere

Mistakes can be forgiven-a lesson to be learned
But this churn of stuff they're handing us, it all needs
    to be burned
All these lies just attract more flies and hurt us where
    we live
They foul the air and make it clear, this is not something
    we can forgive

Evil isn't all the lies we say the Devil tells
It's the heartlessness of man we see, that makes these
    evil smells

6/13/17

The World According to ME

(excerpted quotes from 2018)

"Now is the time for all good men to come to the aid
   of ME "

"I think that I shall never see a poem as lovely as ME"

"Ask not what your country can do for you, ask what
   you can do for ME"

"I'll make America great again, and I'll prove it to you
   and ME,
by sending every one of you to fight and die for ME"

"There is no "I" in team—just ME"

"When your kids grow up they will all want to be ME,
   'The Pussygrabber of the United States'"

"ME doesn't really care how you feel, ME will tell you
   what is real"

"Nothing is better for thee than ME"

"I am the Greatest—not Ali, but ME"

Going Home

She closed the book, placed it on the table, and finally, decided to walk through the door. Roni's hand still throbbed from pounding it on the suitcase to get her boyfriend's attention as she had packed. Well, she got it and now she was out.

The blue and white cab appeared suddenly, noiselessly. It looked brand new. The driver was out of the cab and headed towards her before she even stood up.

"Off to Greyhound?" he said. He had opened the rear door for her and was putting her suitcase in the trunk. She slid in on what felt like leather seats.

"Yeah, thanks, I'm heading . . . hey, how'd you know I was going to the bus station?"

He was already back in the driver's seat hooking up his seatbelt. He turned to her and said with a little smile, "You want to wear yours too, OK?"

"Oh sure, thanks," Roni said. "But how did you . . . "

"What? The bus station? A good cabdriver's like a detective, miss."

Roni had only been in Las Vegas for a few months. Since she didn't have a car, most of her travels had been by cab when she wasn't with her boyfriend. Something about this driver seemed odd.

"Are you sure you're going the right way to the Greyhound station? I'm pretty sure . . . "

"Did you take a cab from the bus station to Budget Suites where I just picked you up?"

"Yes, I did", she said.

"Do you remember how much the cab fare was?"

She had to think. "Uh, . . . it was about twelve dollars. Why?"

"This ride is only going to cost you about seven dollars."

"What? How could that be?"

"'Cause the other driver took you the long way, up on the freeway then off at Sahara, down Industrial to Budget Suites. Lots of drivers do that to make more money."

Come to think of it, she did have a few run-ins like that with some of the cabdrivers. She hadn't thought too much about it though. This driver was different somehow. She was already starting to feel better about leaving her boyfriend and going home.

"Wow, I guess I should thank you for being honest. Sorry for sounding so . . . "

"Hey, not to worry. You had more important things on your mind."

"Well, actually . . . " she stopped. There it was again. How did he know what was on her mind? Now she was curious.

"You seem to be a pretty smart cabby. What do you think I had on my mind?" She saw a tiny smirk appear on his face.

They were just pulling up to the bus station. The meter showed $7.20. As she pulled out the money to pay him, he was already around to open the door with her suitcase in his hand.

"Breaking up is hard to do Veronica, but heading back home is a real good idea."

By the time she remembered the last occasion anyone had called her Veronica, the cab had disappeared.

About the Author

Richard Coletta was born in New Jersey, but grew up all over the United States. He spent most of his life managing restaurants as well as ten years driving a taxi in Las Vegas. He also designed, built and operated his own food cart, and sold Gyros for twelve years in the Pacific Northwest. His latest incarnation is as Mr. Fixit, saving his neighbors loved objects for further enjoyment. Writing has been with him since childhood, though lately he's gotten much better at it.

Made in the USA
Las Vegas, NV
09 August 2021